I0141252

KERNEL OF SANITY

Kermit Frazier

BROADWAY PLAY PUBLISHING INC
New York
www.broadwayplaypublishing.com
info@broadwayplaypublishing.com

First printing: June 2014
Second printing: February 2015
I S B N: 978-0-88145-591-5

Book design: Marie Donovan
Page make-up: Adobe InDesign
Typeface: Palatino
Printed and bound in the U S A

ABOUT THE AUTHOR

Kermit Frazier's plays have been produced in New
York and around the country at such theaters as
the Milwaukee Repertory Theater, Asolo Repertory
Theatre, Seattle Children's Theatre, First Stage
Children's Theater, Baltimore's Centerstage,
the Philadelphia Drama Guild, the Ensemble
Studio Theatre, and the New Federal Theatre.
His plays include KERNEL OF SANITY, DINAH
WASHINGTON IS DEAD, CLASS REUNION,
SHADOWS AND ECHOES, INTERSTICES,
LEGACIES, AN AMERICAN JOURNEY, DREAM
KING, SACRED PLACES, LITTLE ROCK, and
SMOLDERING FIRES. He has also written for such
series as *Gullah Gullah Island* (Co-producer and
Executive Story Editor), *The Cosby Mysteries, The Magic
School Bus, The Misadventures of Maya and Miguel, The
Wonder Pets,* and *All My Children.* He was a creator of
and head writer for the popular children's mystery
series, *Ghostwriter.* "Drive," the first chapter of his
memoir, was published in *Callaloo.* Other articles,
reviews, and short stories have appeared in such
magazines and journals as *Green Mountains Review,
The Chicago Review, American Theatre Magazine, Black
World, Essence,* and *The New York Times Book Review.*
He has had fellowships at the Blue Mountain Center,
MacDowell Colony, Yaddo, Millay Colony, Norton
Island Residency, and the Liguria Study Center for the
Arts and Humanities in Bogliasco, Italy. He teaches
in the M F A Program in Creative Writing at Adelphi
University.

KERNEL OF SANITY was initially given a staged reading at the 1979 National Playwrights Conference of the Eugene O'Neill Memorial Theater Center.

The play subsequently had a production in April, 1985 at the Backdoor Theatre in Wichita Falls, Texas.

The play was produced at New Federal Theatre (Woodie King, Jr, Producer) from 9 April-3 May 2009. The cast and creative contributors were:

FRANK TRACY .... Joel Nagle/*then* Tom Brangle
RITA TEMPLETON .... Madeleine James
ROGER PETERSON .... Chas Reuben

Director .... Petronia Paley
Scenic design .... Pavlo Bosyy
Lighting design .... Shirley Prendergast
Costume design .... Ali Turns
Production stage manager .... Bayo
Assistant Stage Manager .... Rosita Timm
Technical director .... Crystal Scenic Light & Sound/
Anthony Davidson
Casting .... Lawrence Evans

CHARACTERS & SETTING

FRANK TRACY, *White male, early 40s*
RITA TEMPLETON, *White female, early 20s*
ROGER PETERSON, *African American male, early 30s*

The Time: the late 1970s

The Place: a medium-sized town in the Midwest

The action is continuous

(During the preset lighting Steely Dan's "Deacon Blues" plays. As the song begins to fade the preset fades out and lights come up on FRANK, a white man in his early 40s who is dressed in cut-offs, a T-shirt, no shoes or socks, and sitting cross-legged on the sofa. He is writing in a notebook and smoking a cigarette.)

(The room is a cluttered living room. Sofa and coffee table D C, easy chair and hassock D R, armchair D L. Front door entrance is U R on the side wall. Hallway to bedrooms and bathroom is D L and kitchen entrance is U L on side wall. Long table covered with books and papers is in front of windows. Telephone is on that table. End table U R. Floor-to-ceiling bookshelf is U L.)

(The coffee table is cluttered with books, beer and soda cans, papers, envelopes, candy and gum wrappers, a couple of plates, used napkins, a half-filled mug of coffee, books of matches, empty cigarette packages. Clothes and books and papers are scattered everywhere.)

(It's an afternoon in late May in the late 1970s).

(Several seconds after the lights come up FRANK reaches some ending in his writing and drops his cigarette into an empty beer can.)

FRANK: *(Looking through what he's written)* Yeah…yeah.

(FRANK gets up with his notebook and paces around the room, eventually reading aloud from the notebook.)

(His reading will grow more animated as he goes along and will eventually turn into a performance.)

FRANK: I'd had it with L A, see. With everything. I'd
had it with this whole country.... Actually, it came
to me kind of in a flash. I'd driven up to Trousdale
Estates pissed off as hell. I don't know why I used to
do that—drive through Beverly Hills and Trousdale
Estates. I guess the sight of all that decadent luxury
just did something to my blood. I don't know. It was
kind of like getting a fix. I even drove around those
curves once tripping on acid with good ole José. Best
little Chicano actor west of the Rockies. Around and
around like riding those dead animals on a fucking
merry-go-round. Man were we ever gone. And we
drove right up to this huge driveway and parked for
a moment. Sat grooving on these huge ugly striped
drapes these fuckers had for a garage door. A garage
door! And then after a while we backed on out and
drove away. And it was on the way back down that
I missed a curve and almost drove us over a fucking
cliff. Shit, my heart stopped and fucking José screamed.
I could just see us flying over L A like a goddam
Cessna. Flying without wings 'cause we were being
supported by all this dense, gray smog. Yeah, a magic
carpet trip. Hell, we laughed about it for hours.... One
day about two weeks later I went up there for the last
time. I'd been moping around the house, drinking,
reading, trying to write this autobiographical story that
was turning to shit right before my eyes like instant
oatmeal. And Maggie was on the phone gabbing like a
fucking magpie and I was getting pissed off because it
was like I was trapped in an underwater movie. Slow,
wet, gurgly. So I turn on the T V, turn on the news. But
I mean what do I expect, right? I get these actors with
stuck voices and porcelain faces with little cracks for
smiles like they're new mass-produced versions of the
Liberty Bell. And I hear about this important story and
that important story and on and on and on.... So I pick
up this shoe and throw it at the picture of some asshole

that's filling up the screen and sticking to my eyes like silly putty. And the fucking thing blows up. The T V, I mean. A twenty-one inch color T V up in smoke right in the middle of the living room. Man, what a sight. The fucking news of the day. Maggie rushes in all hysterical shouting about bombs like we was in Northern Ireland or something. And when she sees the T V dead and smoking and me just sitting there she starts cursing a blue streak. I try to calm her down by promising to buy her another one, but she cackles and says, "yeah, with whose money?" Then I just get up without saying another word and leave the house. No shoes, no socks, just me and my cigarettes driving my old beat-up V W—which only had a week left to live—up to the hills and Trousdale Estates. And when I get there I park the car on some dry, fire-hungry grass just below a couple of million dollar homes for famous neurotics and look out over the city kind of like those tourists in *The Day of the Locust*. And for the first time I see...nothing. Nothing at all. Oh, I know what's there all right. But somewhere between my eyes and my brain it becomes nothing. And I say to myself: "Frank, it's the end, man." Then it was two more weeks of Zombie City for me—highlighted by several meaningful shouting matches with Maggie. And then back to this town on a Greyhound bus.

(FRANK *reads as he writes.*)

FRANK: Go Midwest, young man. How's that for the beginning of a modern western?

(FRANK *thinks for a moment.*)

FRANK: John Ford eat your heart out!

(FRANK *writes down that last sentence. Then he goes to his cigarette pack on the coffee table and finds it empty.*)

FRANK: Shit.

(FRANK puts his notebook down and begins searching through the things in the living room for more cigarettes.)

(The doorbell rings, but FRANK ignores it. It rings again as he continues his search.)

FRANK: I'm not home. And besides, I don't want any.

(The doorbell rings.)

FRANK: Go away, I said.

(The doorbell rings.)

FRANK: All right, all right. Hang on, dammit.

(FRANK goes to the door and opens it. RITA comes in. She's a white woman in her early 20s who is wearing a skirt and a cotton blouse and is carrying a small purse.)

FRANK: *(Walking away from the door)* Rita.

RITA: Yeah, Rita. I forgot my keys. What were you doing? Sleeping?

FRANK: No, as a matter of fact. I was working.

RITA: Humph.

FRANK: What are you doing here this time of day?

RITA: I got off early.

FRANK: To spy on me?

RITA: No, not to spy on you.

(FRANK continues searching for his cigarettes. RITA sniffs the air.)

RITA: You been doing dope.

FRANK: So?

RITA: And beer.

FRANK: So?

RITA: How much beer?

FRANK: I thought you weren't spying.

RITA: I bet at least a six-pack.

FRANK: You know, it was really peaceful a moment ago. Just a tiny second ago. *(He continues his search.)*

RITA: What the hell are you doing?

FRANK: Have you seen my cigarettes?

RITA: I just got here.

FRANK: I thought sure I had another....

RITA: Does it make sense that I would have seen your cigarettes?

FRANK: Okay, okay.

RITA: Did they walk in with me?

FRANK: All right, already. Jesus, you're a pain in the ass sometimes.

RITA: Try your pants pockets.

FRANK: They ain't in my pants pockets. Don't you think I got sense enough to look in my pockets?

RITA: Well, don't panic, for God's sake. Here, take one of mine.

(RITA takes out a pack of cigarettes, finding that there are only two left. She takes one for herself and tosses the pack to FRANK. They light up. He gets his notebook and sits on the sofa looking through it.)

RITA: *(Sarcastically)* You're welcome.

(FRANK is preoccupied.)

RITA: Frank.

FRANK: *(Without looking up)* What?

(Slight pause)

RITA: Frank, darling.

FRANK: *(Looking up)* What is it?

(RITA *smiles and then goes to* FRANK *and snuggles up to him on the sofa.*)

FRANK: Come on, can't you see I'm working here?

(RITA *begins kissing* FRANK. *At first he resists, but gradually he becomes more and more involved.*)

RITA: Still want me to get off?

FRANK: Well…

(FRANK *and* RITA *continue kissing.*)

FRANK: Let's do it.

RITA: *(Suddenly thrown off)* What?

FRANK: Let's do it.

RITA: When?

FRANK: Now. Right here.

RITA: No.

FRANK: Oh, come on. Nobody's looking.

RITA: No.

FRANK: Why not? I'm up for it.

RITA: 'Cause I've got something really important to talk about.

FRANK: Nonverbal action, baby.

RITA: I'm pregnant.

(FRANK *looks at* RITA *for a moment and then lifts her off his lap and gets up and takes his notebook U S to the table covered with books.*)

RITA: I said I'm pregnant.

FRANK: Yeah.

RITA: And so?

FRANK: What do you mean "and so"?

RITA: And so what are we gonna do?

FRANK: Who knows?

RITA: My daddy's gonna be really pissed.

FRANK: *(Quoting)* "I am not moved to tears."

RITA: What?

FRANK: *The Lion in Winter.*

RITA: Now look—

FRANK: Eleanor says that. Can't remember why, but it sounds appropriate.

RITA: You know I hate that.

FRANK: Carol Stein.

RITA: Frank.

FRANK: Eleanor to my Henry.

RITA: Listen.

FRANK: We were both too young but—

RITA: Stop it!

FRANK: Bitchy broad, that Carol. Kinda like you.

RITA: You sonofabitch.

FRANK: You know I had this dream this morning.

RITA: What?

FRANK: Sometime this morning.

RITA: A dream?

FRANK: I think it was this morning.

RITA: You're gonna tell me about a—

FRANK: What time is it, anyway?

RITA: Now? Now you're gonna tell me about this—

FRANK: It wasn't like any dream I've ever had.

RITA: I really don't wanna hear this right now.

FRANK: But it's relevant. It's really, really relevant.

(Slight pause)

RITA: All right. So you had this dream.

FRANK: Actually, it was kinda like a vision, or a revelation. I'm climbing up this huge, seemingly endless staircase, see, and it's rough, it's really hard, but I keep going, flight after flight after flight, 'cause I know that when I reach the top I'll be right up there. I mean, I'll just have it, I'll be on top. But this is all an illusion, this sense of progress, 'cause every time I manage to climb a flight or two of stairs some fucker with these giant hands picks me up and throws me down a few flights. And this keeps happening until I no longer have the sensation of climbing, no sensation at all of climbing. It's just this thumping sound in my head and bruises forming on my body as I keep being thrown down another flight of stairs.

(RITA just looks at FRANK for a moment.)

RITA: What's your point?

FRANK: My point, dear Rita, is that you being pregnant is just one more kick in the ass as far as I'm concerned, just a perpetuation of the goddam dream.

RITA: No, dear Frank, this ain't no dream I'm talking about here. It's reality. I'm talking about the real thing here.

(FRANK begins to wonder around the room.)

RITA: And now I'm waiting for you to say something real. I'm waiting for some real words to come out of your mouth for a change.

FRANK: Look, I'm sorta tired right now, okay?

RITA: No, uh-uh, none of that. I want some attention paid here, some attention paid to our dilemma.

FRANK: Your dilemma.

RITA: Our dilemma.

FRANK: All right, all right. Then I say good, wonderful. I just love kids. Got three of `em already. Three kids and two divorces. So let me marry you, too, and you can have the kid and we can just get this shit settled 'cause right now I don't want no more hassles, no more thumping sounds.

RITA: Married?

FRANK: Yeah.

RITA: You think I'd marry you, just like that? No questions asked? Get myself permanently hooked up with you just 'cause I'm pregnant. You think that's what I want? Huh? Is that what I want?

FRANK: The woman is mad.

RITA: You've got your nerve.

FRANK: This is a clear case of madness.

RITA: You're really got your nerve.

FRANK: Now wait a minute. Wait just a goddam minute. You come charging in here bitching about some goddam little person growing inside of you and asking me what we should do and when I tell you, you won't even hear it.

(RITA *tries to think of something to say.*)

FRANK: Well, huh, huh? Ain't that the way it went?

RITA: But how can I marry you? How would we live?

FRANK: *(Searching again for cigarettes)* You work, don't you?

RITA: Oh, yeah, sure. And I suppose we'll move into my tiny little apartment with all your books and papers and crap and you'll just keep working on your projects while I bust my ass to keep us alive.

FRANK: You got another cigarette?

RITA: Listen to me.

FRANK: I heard you, dammit. You can come live with me. My father won't kick me out of this place no matter how broke I am. Not as long as he thinks he can keep me in line.... Jesus, do I need a cigarette.

RITA: And do you think I'd come live in this hell hole?

FRANK: You practically live here now.

RITA: It ain't the same.

FRANK: And what do you mean "hell hole"? Three bedrooms, a huge kitchen, a washer and dryer. What more could you ask for?

RITA: A man with a job.

FRANK: Details.

RITA: That's right.

FRANK: Well, I won't need no job once I hear from Social Security.

RITA: You ain't getting nothing from the government. They're not gonna think you're crazy.

FRANK: Mental disability.

RITA: If anyone's crazy it's me for hanging around.

FRANK: Chambers filed an exquisite report.

RITA: He ought to be locked up for malpractice.

FRANK: Well, at least I can hold intelligent conversations with him.

RITA: Oh, yeah? Well, least I know a little bit about living. Least I ain't half-stoned all the time. Least I ain't cooped up in no trashed-out house trying to write some book that I'll probably never finish and that most people probably wouldn't give a shit about anyway.

(FRANK *just looks at* RITA.)

FRANK: I can really do without that now, Rita.

(FRANK *walks away from her. She follows him.*)

RITA: Honey, I'm sorry.

(RITA *hugs* FRANK *from behind.*)

FRANK: Yeah, sure.

RITA: No, I really am. I didn't mean it.

(FRANK *turns and hugs and kisses* RITA. *Then he moves away.*)

FRANK: What a time for you to get pregnant. I was just beginning to make some progress, just beginning to— Shit, I've gotta have some more nicotine in my bloodstream before I die.

(FRANK *exits D L to the bedrooms.* RITA *flops down on the sofa and lets out a huge sigh of relief as though she's just finished an ordeal.*)

RITA: I did it. I actually did it. (*After a moment she has a thought. Calling to* FRANK) Listen, don't you sometimes keep a pack— (*She gets up and goes to the table by the front door to look for cigarettes in its drawer. Finding none, she then begins looking through a stack of mail on the table. Calling to* FRANK *again*) Why don't you ever open your mail?

FRANK: (*Shouting from offstage*) 'Cause it's always either junk or hundred-dollar phone bills.

RITA: (*Calling to* FRANK) They're gonna shut off your phone one day soon.

FRANK: (*Entering*) Let'em. Can I help it if I've got friends all over the country who need me?

RITA: (*Still looking through the mail*) Yeah, your friends need you like a polar bear needs the tropics.

FRANK: (*Combing through junk in the room*) My select friends are my link to sanity in a densely desolate land.

RITA: The only desolation around here is…. *(She discovers a letter from Social Security.)* Oh, Jesus, here it is.

FRANK: What?

RITA: *(Holding the envelope behind her back)* Guess what I found.

FRANK: Ah, shit, I must be blind.

RITA: Guess so.

FRANK: Well, give me one, for Christ's sake. I'm dying here.

RITA: It's not cigarettes I'm holding.

FRANK: Come on, don't play around now.

RITA: What's more important than cigarettes?

FRANK: Nothing.

RITA: Guess again.

(Slight pause)

FRANK: A letter!

RITA: Where?

FRANK: That you're holding behind your back.

RITA: No kidding.

FRANK: Yeah.

(Having stuck the envelope in her skirt behind her back, RITA brings her empty hands around in front of her.)

RITA: I have no idea what you're talking about.

FRANK: Yes, you do.

(FRANK chases RITA around the living room. When he catches her he grabs the envelope from out of her skirt and moves D C in front of the sofa.)

FRANK: My God, the Social Security Administration. *(He stares at the envelope.)*

RITA: So open it, already.

FRANK: Do you realize what this could mean?

RITA: Yeah. If it's yes, you're crazy. If it's no, you'll go crazy.

FRANK: I could either work in peace or go down the drain. *(He opens the envelope quickly and lets it drop to the floor as he reads the letter.)*

RITA: What does it say?

FRANK: Huh?

RITA: What does the letter say?

FRANK: Rita, your daddy's gonna shit in his pants when he finds out that you're gonna be married to a government certified cretin.

(RITA rushes to FRANK and hugs him.)

RITA: Honey, that's terrific.

(FRANK dances around the room.)

FRANK: Sonofabitch.

RITA: Jesus, what am I saying?

FRANK: It's a godsend, that's what it is. This is it. The end to all my problems. It's to the top, all the way to the top. No more thump, thump, thump on the ole stairs.

RITA: Yeah, thump, thump.

FRANK: I should call him right now. Call up good buddy Chambers. What a shrink!

(FRANK goes U C to the phone.)

RITA: He probably already knows, the quack.

FRANK: Call him up and give him the biggest telephone kiss he's ever had. What a genius! What a fucking genius!

(The doorbell rings.)

RITA: That's probably him at the door. Coming to claim his percentage.

(FRANK dials the phone. RITA goes to the door and opens it. In the doorway is ROGER, a black man in his early 30s. He is dressed in slacks and a sports shirt and carries a shoulder bag.)

ROGER: Does Frank Tracy live here?

RITA: Uh, yeah. Yeah, he lives here. Frank.

FRANK: What?

RITA: Somebody here to see you.

FRANK: Good.

RITA: Come on in. He's on the phone right now.

(ROGER comes in and RITA closes the door. ROGER is somewhat shocked by the chaotic nature of the room. Then he looks directly at FRANK. RITA waits at the door behind ROGER.)

FRANK: *(Into the phone)* Look, Chambers, you beautiful sonofabitch, this is you know who. And I just wanna say thanks and give you a big ole kiss. *(He kisses the phone.)* And if you can't guess why, then just give me a call. *(He slams down the phone.)* I hate those fucking machines.

RITA: Frank.

FRANK: What?

RITA: You got company.

ROGER: Hey, Frank.

FRANK: *(Slightly puzzled)* Oh…hi.

ROGER: You mean you don't remember me?

(FRANK stares at ROGER for a long moment.)

FRANK: Oh my God. I don't believe it. *Cuckoo's Nest.*

ROGER: Right.

FRANK: One of the aides.

ROGER: Yeah.

FRANK: Now wait a minute, wait a minute. Don't tell me. I'm usually good at this. Roger. Roger Peterson.

ROGER: Yeah.

FRANK: Roger Peterson.

RITA: He said "yeah."

FRANK: Well, I'll be goddamed. *(He rushes to* ROGER *and gives him a big hug and kiss.)* Jesus Christ, ole buddy, what the hell are you doing here?

ROGER: Well, I—

FRANK: Honey, it's Roger.

RITA: I know.

FRANK: Christ, it's been what? Three years?

ROGER: Four.

FRANK: Four? Jesus. Well, come on in. Sit down. What the hell are you doing here? How'd you even find this place?

ROGER: Well, I'm on my way to the West Coast. And I thought: what the hell. I'll get off the freeway and—

FRANK: Yeah, but how'd you know I was here? How'd you get my address?

ROGER: Oh, uh…Morris Hathaway.

FRANK: Hathaway? Don't tell me you know him.

ROGER: I met him at this party and…well, your name came up. Eventually.

FRANK: He produced this post *Easy Rider*, seventies, noir shit of a picture I was in. The director was an asshole but what you gonna do? Man, it's such a trip that you're here. And you look so good, too.

ROGER: Think so?

FRANK: As good as ever. Not a day older in four years. Don't he still look good, honey?

RITA: I guess. What do I know?

FRANK: Hey, I'm sorry. Roger, this is Rita. Rita Templeton. Rita, Roger.

(RITA *and* ROGER *shake hands awkwardly.*)

ROGER: Hi.

RITA: Hi.

FRANK: Well, sit down, sit down. *(He pushes papers and junk off the sofa and onto the floor.)* Sorry about the mess. Been too busy lately to clean up.

RITA: *(To herself)* Yeah, busy.

FRANK: You understand.

ROGER: *(Sitting)* Sure.

(RITA *sits D R in the easy chair.*)

FRANK: Man, what a surprise. Two fucking fantastic surprises in a row. And what timing. An official aide straight from the Cuckoo's Nest. Just what I need now. Right, Rita?

RITA: Sure, Frank.

FRANK: Sorta completes the illusion. Makes it real as can be.

ROGER: What illusion?

RITA: Frank's gonna—

FRANK: And I just knew it. I just knew things had to be looking up. *(Quoting)* "Been down so long it looks like up to me."

RITA: Frank.

FRANK: Richard Fariña. Joan Baez's sister Mimi's writer/husband dude. Man, did he know how to live. And what a way to go! When I go it's gonna be something like that. Racing toward oblivion on a fucking motorcycle. Me and Fariña and Duane Allman and Berry Oakley. Leaving our names behind like skid marks on a fucking expressway. Deacon Bluesin' it all out with—

RITA: Frank, let him talk.

FRANK: What?

RITA: Give him a chance to talk.

FRANK: Oh, yeah… The "Left Coast," huh? On your way to good ole "Hell-A."

ROGER: Yeah.

FRANK: New York finally did it to you, huh?

ROGER: Let's just say that—

FRANK: Honey, you got a cigarette?

RITA: No, I don't.

FRANK: Roger?

ROGER: Sorry, I don't smoke.

FRANK: Yeah, nasty habit. *(To* RITA*)* Honey, how about going to the store and getting us some cigarettes?

*(*RITA *gets up slowly.)*

FRANK: No, wait. I'll go.

RITA: Don't be silly. You got company.

FRANK: Who? Roger? Shit, he ain't company. Besides, I need the walk. I can't keep still.

RITA: Why don't you take my car?

FRANK: For three or four blocks?

RITA: You'll get back sooner.

FRANK: Nah, I need the walk. *(He searches for his shoes.)*

RITA: You sure you don't want me to go?

FRANK: No, dammit. I said no.

RITA: Okay, okay.

(FRANK finds his shoes and slips them on without socks.)

FRANK: Jesus, do I need a smoke.

RITA: Get some vanilla wafers, will you?

FRANK: I'm buying cigarettes.

RITA: So just turn left before you get to the counter and pick up one of those boxes that's got "vanilla wafers" written all over it.

FRANK: And beer. Got to get some beer. Hell, we've gotta celebrate. It's celebration time.

RITA: Vanilla wafers, okay?

FRANK: I'm buying cigarettes and beer.

RITA: Please.

FRANK: I'm buying cigarettes and beer.

RITA: Frank.

FRANK: *(Checking his pockets)* All right, all right... Honey, you got any money?

ROGER: I've got some.

FRANK: No, you've got a long way to go still.

RITA: *(Going to her purse)* How the hell were you gonna buy cigarettes and beer without any money?

FRANK: Grief. All I get is grief.

RITA: *(Handing FRANK some money)* Buy a carton.

FRANK: *(Kissing her)* That's my babe.

RITA: And bring back my change. That's two twenties there.

FRANK: Community property.

RITA: Not yet, darling.

FRANK: Soon enough.

RITA: Don't hold your breath.

FRANK: *(To* ROGER*)* Be right back.

(As FRANK *heads for the door,* ROGER *suddenly stands up quickly.)*

ROGER: Frank.

FRANK: *(Turning back to* ROGER*)* Yeah?

*(*ROGER *stares at* FRANK *for a moment.)*

ROGER: It's really good to see you, man.

FRANK: Yeah, same here, same here. Look, I won't be a minute. Sit down. Make yourself at home. *(To* RITA*)* And don't you tell him.

RITA: Tell him what?

FRANK: Anything.

RITA: I won't say a word.

FRANK: 'Cause I wanna tell him.

RITA: I won't say a word.

FRANK: *(To* ROGER*)* She'll talk your head off.

RITA: I won't.

FRANK: Just see that you don't.

RITA: Will you just go, for God's sake.

*(*FRANK *goes to the door again.)*

RITA: Don't forget my vanilla wafers.

*(*FRANK *exits without responding, slamming the door behind him.)*

RITA: I bet he forgets. His mind is like a sieve when it's convenient.

(RITA *and* ROGER *look at each other for an awkward moment.*)

RITA: Cuckoo's Nest?

ROGER: It's a play. *One Flew Over the Cuckoo's Nest.*

RITA: Oh. So who flew over it? You or Frank?

ROGER: *(With an ironic laugh)* Neither one of us, actually.

RITA: Yeah, well, at least he's consistent.

ROGER: I beg your pardon?

(RITA *quickly remembers that she's not supposed to tell* ROGER *about* FRANK's *resent "fortune".)*

RITA: Oh, uh, nothing. *(Eager to change the subject)* So you and Frank were close, huh?

ROGER: In a way, yes.

RITA: Funny, he's never mentioned you.

ROGER: Well…he had a lotta friends in New York.

RITA: Yeah, but the way he talks… Listen, I'm sorry. I'm being so rude. Can I get you something? I don't think there's much but I'll check.

ROGER: Just a cold glass of water would be fine.

RITA: You sure you don't want nothing else?

ROGER: No, really, just the water.

RITA: Okay, coming right up.

(RITA *exits U L into the kitchen.* ROGER *stares after her. Then he thinks for a moment. He looks around and then gets up and begins to explore the room, looking through papers, books, etc. He is a little on edge, and it's as though his exploration is an attempt both to orient and to calm himself.)*

(RITA *enters with a glass of water and watches* ROGER *for a moment as he looks through a book.*)

RITA: It's junk.

ROGER: *(Turning to* RITA*)* Really?

RITA: Well, most of it. To me at least. Here you are.

(RITA *gives* ROGER *the glass of water.*)

ROGER: Thanks. *(He drinks the water and then continues looking through* FRANK's *books, his shoulder bag still draped from his shoulder.*)

RITA: It's a good thing you didn't want anything else. All I found that was halfway edible was a jar of peanut butter and a couple of grapefruits. *(Adding quickly)* Of course, it's not always like that. I take care of him.

ROGER: *(Nodding)* Hmm.

(ROGER *is looking through a book.* RITA *tries to think of something else to say. Finally…*)

RITA: Frank's a nut about books. That is, about having them around. I don't know how many of 'em he's actually read but he likes having them around. I like to read some, too, but having them around is another matter altogether. Especially if you've already read them. I mean, what's the use of having a load of books around if you've already—

(RITA *stops her line of reasoning when she realizes that* ROGER *is deep into one of the books.*)

RITA: What are you reading?

ROGER: *(Putting the book down)* I'm sorry. Pretty rude of me.

RITA: That's okay.

(ROGER *begins wandering around the room.*)

RITA: Jesus, Frank shouldn't have left you like this.

ROGER: No, that's all right. I'm used to it. Makes me feel right at home.

RITA: What does?

ROGER: Waiting. You see, actors are always waiting. Waiting to be seen, waiting to go on, waiting to get "discovered." So waiting makes me feel right at home.

RITA: Oh.

(ROGER *moves slowly D S away from* RITA.)

ROGER: I even used to wait backstage for Frank. That is, wait to see him go on as McMurphy. Stick my eye up to this tiny little chink in one of the walls of the set. It was so small you could hardly see it from a distance, and yet through it everything on stage was so magnified, so crystal clear.... I'd watch him work, watch how he moved, behaved, instinctively responded to everyone, everything. It was magic, what he did. Magic. It was so exciting that I sometimes.... And the part I had was so small, so nothing. Just an aide. Only an aide. Hardly a line of dialogue. So what else was there to do but just wait and wait and wait?

(*Slight pause*)

(RITA *eyes* ROGER's *shoulder bag.*)

RITA: You can put your bag down, you know. This here's one of them safe neighborhoods.

(ROGER *stares at* RITA *but doesn't set his bag down.*)

RITA: (*With a nervous laugh*) That was a joke.

(ROGER *says nothing.*)

RITA: Actually, you don't see guys carrying bags like that in this town. 'Cause I mean, this isn't the most liberal, up-to-date, open town in the world, you know. Me and Frank have problems enough. Especially Frank. He grew up here, but he left cursing everybody when he was about seventeen so nobody can

understand why he all of a sudden decided to settle
back here after all those wild years as an actor—

ROGER: *(Taken aback)* You say he settled back here?

RITA: Yeah, don't that beat all?

ROGER: But Hathaway said…

RITA: Something wrong?

ROGER: No. I just thought he was still based on
the West Coast. I though this was just some sort of
vacation. Down time.

RITA: Nah. He claims he's not acting anymore. That is,
not like you anyway.

*(ROGER is still trying to wrap his head around the idea that
FRANK might have permanently fled from the West Coast.)*

RITA: Are you a star or something?

ROGER: Huh? Oh, nah, I'm more like a comet.

(RITA is puzzled.)

ROGER: That was a joke.

(RITA remembers her attempt at cover.)

RITA: Well, I mean, have I seen you on T V or in the
movies?

ROGER: Not in anything you'd remember.

RITA: Frank's done lots of T V.

ROGER: I know.

RITA: I've seen him a couple of times. He looked so
dumpy. I said, Frank, what did they do to you? And he
just said, it's T V, Rita, it's T V. Whatever the hell that
means. *(Pause)* It's funny that Frank's never mentioned
you. 'Cause he's such a fanatic about his true friends.
It's Michael this, Michael that. And Andy, Andy,
Andy. And if I could just see Gloria and Tommy again.
And guess who called me last night, all the way from

Venice—the one in California, I mean. José! Well, what
am I supposed to do, jump for joy? I say, José who?
Then he gets mad 'cause he remembers that I don't
know. And so I say, if José's so goddam important
to you how come you ain't in California with him? I
mean, I didn't ask him to come back here. Hell, I didn't
even know him until about six months ago. *(Slight
pause)* But he's never talked about you.

ROGER: *(Essentially to himself)* Maybe he never had any
real reason to.

(Having ignored ROGER's *remark,* RITA *just looks at him for
a moment.)*

RITA: Can I ask you a question?

ROGER: Sure.

RITA: Well...were you and Frank ever...lovers?

ROGER: *(A little taken aback)* Lovers? You mean as in...

RITA: Yeah. *(Quickly)* Now don't get me wrong.

ROGER: I don't think I'm getting you wrong.

RITA: 'Cause if you were it's okay with me.

ROGER: But we weren't.

RITA: And it fits in with this theory of mine.

ROGER: I said we weren't.

RITA: It's okay. Really. You see, I figure that the reason
Frank can never stay with one woman long, why he's
always starting families and then getting divorces and
all, is because he's so in love with himself that other
people just keep getting in the way. So although he
needs women to be with and be taken care of and stuff
it never works for long because he's almost always
got this mirror right in front of his face that keeps him
from being able to see other people. You follow?

ROGER: I think so.

RITA: But men are different. And knowing Frank I figure that he's tried with them too since at least they come closer to looking like him.

(ROGER *just looks at* RITA.)

RITA: Well, in a way. And since he's spent most of his life around strange theater people he's had plenty of chances to try a few men. I mean, it makes sense, doesn't it?

ROGER: If you say so.

RITA: And maybe that's why he's never mentioned you.

ROGER: Oh, I see.

RITA: Except I've never told Frank about all this because he'd just get pissed off. So don't tell him I asked you.

ROGER: I won't.

RITA: But I just figured I'd bring it up and see how it fit in with my theory.

ROGER: But we weren't lovers.

RITA: Okay.

ROGER: No, really. I'm not gay. Or even bi.

RITA: Oh, I know. And it's okay, really. Hell, you shouldn't have to be anything in particular. I mean, people are what they are whenever they need to be it. But you shouldn't have to be anything in particular. And it doesn't bother me really or I wouldn't be who I am. And I damn sure wouldn't be with Frank. You know, most people in this town don't give two shits about me or Frank. And as far as I'm concerned they can all just shove it.... You've heard of Janis Joplin, right?

ROGER: Of course.

RITA: Well, that's me. Sort of. I even look a little bit like her if you squint.

ROGER: Squint?

RITA: Yeah.

(ROGER *squints and then unsquints.*)

RITA: Well?

ROGER: Uh…no.

RITA: Nothing?

ROGER: I'm sorry.

RITA: Well, sometimes…. Anyway, I read this article about her once. She grew up a misfit. All throughout her childhood people kept stepping on her face. So she became a singer. And when she sings I can just feel her talking to me. I know what she's saying. It's almost like I can creep inside her skin and live there and it would be a perfect fit. You know what I mean?

ROGER: Yeah. Smokey Robinson.

RITA: Huh?

ROGER: It used to be Smokey Robinson for me. Smokey Robinson and the Miracles. When I was growing up I was so in love with those records that sometimes I'd hear his voice in my sleep. It was so strange. I never understood what it meant then. What that feeling meant. Or maybe I was just afraid. Something outside of yourself penetrating you right to the bone.

RITA: *(With a knowing smile)* Yeah. You and Smokey, me and Janis…. Goddam creeps. High school phonies… You've seen pictures of Janis Joplin, right? So you know that "plain" is a nice word for how she looked. But she showed them. She showed all those Miss Teenage Texas fluff heads. And when she sings. Jesus. It's skin to skin. Just that close.

ROGER: *(In his own memory)* Yeah, I heard that.

(For a moment RITA *and* ROGER *are frozen in position, neither of them facing the other. Then she comes out of it.)*

RITA: But sometimes I wonder what difference it finally makes. I mean, I've got this job, see, where all I do is type letters and forms and answer the phone all day and announce people. "So-and-so is here to see you, sir." "I'm sorry, So-and-so, but he's on another line." I'm like this filter, see. This filter on this cigarette. And somehow it just doesn't seem fair. I mean, all you really get is dirty. Other people's dirt passing through you like nothing about you really counted.

ROGER: And so then it becomes like oozing. Like oozing outside of yourself to find out who you are.

RITA: I beg your pardon.

ROGER: Or like trying to stretch your skin so tightly over someone else's image that you feel you just might be able to absorb them.

*(*RITA *thinks about this for a moment.)*

RITA: Oh, yeah...Janis.

ROGER: Frank.

RITA: Huh?

*(*FRANK *bursts through the door with two bags in his arms and a cigarette dangling from his mouth.)*

FRANK: Roger, you ole sonofabitch. So New York did you in, huh?

ROGER: Excuse me.

FRANK: What you been doing? Soaps?

ROGER: I don't know what you're—

FRANK: 'Course, I never did one. Too confining. And all that repetitious, melodramatic doubletalk. I told Skeeter, my agent, not to even come at me with that shit. Still, why didn't you tell me? And what's waiting for you in Hollywood? A series? A movie deal?

RITA: *(To* ROGER*)* It must be the fresh air. He hasn't been out in days.

FRANK: No, it's the red Camaro, Rita. Roger's driving a brand new fucking red Camaro convertible.

ROGER: Oh, that.

FRANK: Shit, yeah, "oh that".

ROGER: Just a gift to myself. It's a long story.

FRANK: I got time.

ROGER: No, really. I'd rather not talk about it just yet.

FRANK: Okay, okay. But I'm holding you to it, you sneaky sonofabitch. Anyway, I stopped by the liquor store for some real booze. *(He sets the bags on the U C table and begins taking things out of them.)* A real celebration. A fifth of gin. Some tonic water. A six-pack of Coors. A carton of Benson & Hedges. A bunch of Frito's Doritos. Some nose-opening salsa. And...vanilla wafers.

RITA: You got'em.

FRANK: *(To* ROGER*)* She thought I'd forget.

RITA: Well, your mind is...

FRANK & RITA: ...like a sieve when it's convenient.

FRANK: That's what I love about her, Roger. Her utter, inimitable originality.

RITA: *(Opening package of vanilla wafers)* Go to hell, Frank.

FRANK: I bet she talked your head off.

RITA: I did not.

ROGER: No, she didn't.

FRANK: Well, how about a beer? Or a stiff gin and tonic?

ROGER: First I'd like to use your bathroom.

FRANK: Sure, sure. Through there and to your right.

ROGER: Thanks. *(He exits D L with his shoulder bag.)*

FRANK: *(Calling after ROGER)* And don't mind the shit. None of it's dangerous.

RITA: *(Admonishingly)* Jesus, Frank.

FRANK: *(Sitting down on the sofa)* Man, am I tired.

RITA: *(Eating vanilla wafers)* You should've taken my car.

FRANK: I should've taken his car. Anyway, I needed the exercise and the sun. I'm getting pale as a ghost. Too much time cooped up in this goddam place.

(FRANK takes a stash of marijuana out of a covered bowl on the coffee table and begins putting some in a pipe. RITA is preoccupied with thought.)

FRANK: Guess who I ran into at the liquor store.

RITA: Who?

FRANK: Fletcher.

RITA: Oh.

FRANK: He says to me: "I thought you'd be dead by now".

RITA: That's nice.

FRANK: What a thing to say to a guy you used to practically share barstools with. I almost decked the sonofabitch right there.

RITA: *(Barely listening)* Good.

FRANK: "All my friends are gonna be strangers." Yeah, that says it, all right. I wanted to tell Fletcher right there. Tell him: just watch what you say 'cause you're talking to a crazy man who's got his shit together now, if you know what I mean.

RITA: Uh-huh. *(Slight pause)* Frank.

FRANK: What?

RITA: I don't like it.

FRANK: Like what?

RITA: I think there's something wrong.

FRANK: With what?

RITA: With your friend Roger there.

FRANK: What the hell are you talking about?

RITA: I tell you there's something wrong.

FRANK: No, there isn't.

RITA: Yes, there is.

FRANK: What, then? What's wrong? What happened?

RITA: Well...nothing. It's just that...I can just feel it.

FRANK: No, you can't. You just don't know him, that's all.

RITA: I wonder what he's doing here.

FRANK: He came to see me.

RITA: I bet he's on downers. Don't it seem like he's on downers?

FRANK: Rita, will you stop. Maybe he's just tired. Besides, it could have been you, you know. What the hell did you say to him? Did you tell him?

RITA: No.

FRANK: 'Cause I wanted to tell him.

RITA: So tell him, for God's sake.

FRANK: And keep quiet about you being pregnant.

RITA: Huh?

FRANK: Pregnant, pregnant. You know, your big news of the day.

RITA: Yeah, sure. *(Slight pause)* He's been in there a long time. Don't you think you should see if he's all right?

FRANK: See? What see? Why? Maybe he's taking a shit or something.

RITA: Jesus.

FRANK: Well, if you're so worried about him why don't you go see.

(The sound of the toilet flushing.)

FRANK: See? Now just shut up. And act civilized, for God's sake.

RITA: Humph, you should talk.

FRANK: Yeah, well...

RITA: What we've got here is your own personal jungle.

FRANK: And after we're married you can help me blaze right on through it.

RITA: The fuck I will.

(ROGER enters. FRANK offers up the pipe.)

FRANK: Roger, baby, have a toke.

ROGER: No, thanks.

FRANK: Oh, come on.

ROGER: Maybe later.

FRANK: So sit down, sit down. What'll you have? A beer? Gin?

ROGER: Gin. *(He sits D R on the sofa and places his shoulder bag on the floor next to it.)*

FRANK: Good. Honey—

RITA: Yeah, I know.

FRANK: Two gin and tonics.

RITA: Three. *(She takes things into the kitchen.)*

FRANK: She keeps me alive, man. Keeps me from doing too many terrible things to myself.... But hey, what's going on with you? What's been happening? How's New York?

ROGER: Worse. Kinda bankrupt, actually.

FRANK: Shit, the whole damn country's kinda bankrupt. Really on the skids. That's one reason why I'm holed up here. Just trying to keep out of the line of fire. 'Cause they're after us.

ROGER: Who is?

FRANK: The assholes. They're all out to get the few of us left who still have brains and imagination. You see, it's like this. I've got this thing about entropy. You know, like the Second Law of Thermodynamics, heat-death, loss of energy, physics applied to social shit.

ROGER: Chaos.

FRANK: Disorganization, sameness.

ROGER: Things running down.

FRANK: Yeah, that's it, that's it.... Us, man. You and me. You know, I just had a feeling you'd understand.... And so my objective now is to remain on the edge of things so that I won't be consumed while at the same time preparing myself for when the fog lifts—if it ever does. Preparing myself mostly by reading and writing. It's important to keep your brain active. That's the key.

(ROGER laughs.)

FRANK: What's so funny?

ROGER: For a moment there you sounded a little like my father.

FRANK: *(Sarcastically)* Jesus, thanks a lot.

ROGER: No, really. He used to lecture me when I was a kid about keeping my brain active.

FRANK: Well, you know what I mean.

ROGER: Yeah, I know. But he made it sound like some sort of categorical imperative. And when I left for New York to study acting his biggest argument against it was that my brain would rot.

(FRANK *eyes* ROGER *playfully.)*

FRANK: Well, has it?

ROGER: No more than other things, I guess.

FRANK: Yeah, I hear you. So listen, honestly, what's up? You been doing Broadway or something?

ROGER: Naw, not really. I did do this off-Broadway thing, though. A revival of Richard Wright's *Native Son.* The Paul Green stage adaptation. Huh, ole man Green himself even came to the show.

FRANK: Wow. So how was it playing Bigger Thomas?

ROGER: Bigger Thomas? Shit, I wish. I was Jack, one of his buddies. A step up from a *Cuckoo's Nest* aide, though.

FRANK: Yeah, climbing that ole ladder of success.

ROGER: I was in the running to be Bigger. *(With an ironic smirk)* Huh. To do bigger and better things. All came down to type, perception.

FRANK: Tell me about it.

ROGER: Fear, flight, fate.

FRANK: *(Glibly, not getting the reference to* Native Son*)* Don't forget "fucked."

(ROGER *simply smiles.)*

FRANK: And then after that what—

ROGER: *(Quickly deflecting)* Kelly's on Broadway, though.

FRANK: Who?

ROGER: Kelly Mackin.

FRANK: Shit, no, not Kelly.

ROGER: Square business.

FRANK: Good ole Mister Mumbles.

ROGER: You got it.

FRANK: I had to kick Finkelstein's ass three times to get him to get Kelly to speak up.

ROGER: I remember.

FRANK: Just because Billy Babbitt stutters don't mean he can't speak up. "It's my method," he said. Hell, it was like trying to communicate with a guppy or something.

ROGER: Yeah, it was a trip.

FRANK: Assholes. Ninety-eight percent of them are one hundred percent asshole.

ROGER: Remember that night at Phebe's?

FRANK: Oh, man, do I ever.

ROGER: Kelly jumps up to stop Lonnie and Alton from going at each other over some stupid shit and knocks a full glass of beer right into Alton's lap.

FRANK: And so then Alton grabs Kelly and goes to dump his glass of wine spritzer over his head before I step in.

ROGER: "It's not my fault," Kelly shouts.

FRANK: "It's always your fault," Alton shouts back.

FRANK & ROGER: "That's your character, man, your fucking character."

(FRANK *and* ROGER *laugh together.*)

FRANK: He fuckin' never knew when to come out behind it all. To just let it go.

(After a moment their laughter dies. Then FRANK *wraps an arm around* ROGER.*)*

FRANK: I had a fuckin' ball doing *Cuckoo's Nest*. I really did.

ROGER: *(Moving out of* FRANK's *grasp)* I guess so. It was all you.

FRANK: What do you mean?

ROGER: You, Frank. You took the stage. You ran with the ball.

FRANK: Yeah, well, I'm a good ole quarterback from way back, you know.

ROGER: The power and the glory.

FRANK: Abso-fucking-lutely.

(FRANK *laughs heartily again, but this time* ROGER *doesn't.*)

ROGER: *(Soberly)* Back then anyway.

(FRANK *looks curiously at* ROGER, *perhaps remembering what* RITA *has been saying, but then quickly lets it go.*)

FRANK: Man, Kelly didn't have no talent. Or better yet: his talent was negative. He had to sap other people just to make it to zero. Slurp, slurp.

ROGER: I guess that's what it was then.

FRANK: I'm sure it was.

ROGER: Me and Kelly trying to pull ourselves up, trying to raise the level to zero.

FRANK: What the hell are you talking about? I'm not equating you with Kelly.

ROGER: I'm on my way to the Coast.

FRANK: But you're not Kelly. You're not. I know phoniness when I see it. Kelly's a fuck-face, a simpleton. And I know you're not that. So let's just keep the proper perspective here.

ROGER: *(With a playful smirk)* Well, in that case, actually it's just an understudy thing.

FRANK: For you?

ROGER: No, for Kelly.

FRANK: Oh, well, shit, that's a little better. As long as he don't have to act much on a regular basis. Phoniness. Leave it to the Kellies, man. Although, frankly, I don't know how much reality you're gonna find on the West Coast either. The bullshit's just as thick as it is in New York.... "Cabalistic enclaves dot the California landscape like postulating pimples."

ROGER: Who said that?

FRANK: I don't know. I read it in gas station john in Santa Barbara. And so I got out a pen and wrote right below it: "The last frontier scarred for life". Shit, just one more bit of information to jam up the system. You see, I spent months there just trying to deal with things, just trying to keep afloat. Then I married a rich broad and started a theater with her money. We did a few shows. Shakespeare, O'Neill, Albee. But that didn't last long because the union got hot over us "occasionally" breaking their rules and regulations and forced us to close down. But you know what it was, don't you? The art. They couldn't handle the art. "Artistic" is pronounced another way in most places.

(RITA comes in with three gin and tonics, a bowl of Doritos, salsa dip, vanilla wafers, and peanut butter on a tray.)

ROGER: How's it pronounced?

FRANK: "Autistic." Anything beyond autism simply confuses people.

RITA: *(Setting tray on coffee table)* Who're you talking about?

FRANK: You, honey.

RITA: Yeah, I bet. *(To ROGER)* It's all lies. I don't think Frank's told the truth in years.

FRANK: Hyperbolic recriminations.

RITA: And what the hell's that supposed to mean?

FRANK: *(To ROGER)* Words make her nervous.

RITA: Go to hell, Frank.

FRANK: Rita, some things are true even if they never happened.

RITA: Don't quote shit to me.

FRANK: *(To ROGER)* A variation on Ken Kesey.

RITA: *(To ROGER)* I hate it when he does that.

FRANK: Actually, I think it's kind of appropriate under the circumstances. Don't you, Roger?

RITA: I always say if you can't use your own words then you should just keep quiet.

(Everyone is silent for a moment.)

RITA: Well, help yourselves. This is as far as I go.

(They each take a glass and a few snacks. RITA takes the vanilla wafers and begins to spread peanut butter on them. FRANK and ROGER just watch her for a moment.)

RITA: So did you tell him?

FRANK: No. Just give me a chance, will you? ...Roger, baby, I've brought the Cuckoo's Nest right to my own little place of abode. I've become a precious, priceless fruitcake. Nature's nut of the hour. The government's most fortunate freak.

ROGER: I don't understand.

RITA: He means that the government's gonna send him mental disability checks and he's not even crazy.

FRANK: Rita.

RITA: Leastwise, not the way they think.

FRANK: Rita! Will you just be quiet and let me talk? *(Back to* ROGER*)* Anyway, it's like this. I've been in and out of psychiatrists' offices much of my life. A real yo-yo trip. Kinda like Benny Profane on the Times Square, Grand Central shuttle in Pynchon's novel *V.* Everybody trying to figure me out. My parents could never understand why I wasn't cute and quiet like my two older brothers. My teachers could never understand why I couldn't follow directions. My Calvinistic minister could never understand why I hated God so much—and even I didn't know where the hell he got that idea. Shit, I've been diagnosed by everybody. Diagnosed as—

RITA: Frank.

FRANK: What?

RITA: Just tell him, honey.

FRANK: Yeah. *(Back to* ROGER*)* So anyway, me and Maggie only stayed together in L A two years.

RITA: Frank.

FRANK: I'm getting to it. *(Back to* ROGER*)* She split for Sausalito, back to her lazy luxury. And I took the little bit of money that she left me and ended up here. Back home. Where my parents let me rent their old house cheap to get me off their backs and where I met crazy Rita.

RITA: Yeah, crazy.

FRANK: And a beautiful crazy shrink named Walter Chambers, who reads the kind of stuff I read, likes to

talk to me about my ideas, and regularly supplies me
with Ritalin, no questions asked.

ROGER: What's Ritalin?

FRANK: An anti-depressant, an upper. For adults,
anyway. Kinda like speed.

RITA: As if he doesn't do enough dope.

FRANK: It's called a "prescription drug", Rita.

RITA: It's still dope.

FRANK: Then Chambers got this beautiful idea.
Since I'd been in a sanatorium a couple of times,
why not apply for mental disability? He helped me
file the application and I just got approval from the
government today. I get a monthly check as long as I
report periodically for a mental checkup. So as long as
I just act crazy every once in a while I'm set for life.

ROGER: I don't believe it.

RITA: It's true.

FRANK: So now I'm free.

ROGER: But can that happen?

RITA: I guess.

FRANK: Free to get on with my work.

ROGER: I don't understand this.

RITA: Me neither.

FRANK: No more hassles.

RITA: So he thinks.

FRANK: Now I can clear the air.

RITA: You'll clear the air, all right.

FRANK: My book will clear the air.

RITA: You'll be lucky if you manage to just clear this
room.

FRANK: Rita doesn't understand me sometimes.

RITA: A lotta times.

FRANK: She thinks—inasmuch as she can—that I'm wasting my time.

RITA: Go to hell, Frank.

FRANK: She's also a poor judge of contraceptives.

RITA: That's enough, Frank.

ROGER: *(Rising suddenly from his chair)* Wait a minute.... So that's what you meant? *Cuckoo's Nest* revisited.

FRANK: Yeah, sort of.

ROGER: With me fitting right in again. An "aide" to your illusion, so to speak.

FRANK: You know what I meant.

ROGER: And it's so perfect.

FRANK: Ain't it, though? An airtight solution.

RITA: Airtight, all right. Just wait 'til he goes for his checkup.

FRANK: I'm a damn good actor, Rita.

ROGER: *(Setting down his drink)* Let's do a scene, Frank.

FRANK: Huh?

ROGER: Let's do a scene together.

FRANK: When?

ROGER: Now.

FRANK: Why?

ROGER: 'Cause you're a damn good actor.

FRANK: No.

RITA: Oh, go on, Frank. I'd love to see you do a scene.

FRANK: No.

RITA: *(To* ROGER*)* You know, I've never seen him on stage.

ROGER: Good.

FRANK: I don't want to.

ROGER: Oh, come on. It's perfect. You, me. We'll go back to *Cuckoo's Nest*, since we're halfway there anyway.

RITA: I'm gonna love this.

FRANK: *(To* RITA*)* I said no.

ROGER: Come on, Frank.

FRANK: Hey, now look—

ROGER: Well, I did go out of my way to pay you a visit, didn't I? So the least you can do is do a scene with me, for old time's sake.

RITA: He's right, Frank. That's the least you can do.

FRANK: What is this, a conspiracy or something? Did you two plan this while I was out buying vanilla wafers?

ROGER: No, it just occurred to me.

*(*FRANK *looks at* RITA *and* ROGER *for a moment.)*

FRANK: All right, all right.

RITA: Hooray!

FRANK: Rita, if you're gonna act like a peanut gallery we can just forget it.... Okay, Roger, a scene. I'll see if I can find the script.

ROGER: Don't bother, it's in my head.

FRANK: Well, it ain't in mine.

ROGER: I know. I haven't written it yet.

FRANK: But I thought you said *Cuckoo's Nest*.

ROGER: An out-take. This is sort of like an out-take.

FRANK: What is this, Roger?

RITA: What's an out-take?

FRANK: Dead video.

ROGER: Discarded video.

RITA: Huh?

FRANK: How the hell can a play have an out-take?

ROGER: Well...background then. Behind the scenes. Color.

FRANK: Now look—

ROGER: Just trust me, okay? Remember, you're safe now. Free.

RITA: This is sorta crazy all of a sudden.

ROGER: No, it's sane. It's very, very sane. (*He begins to pace.*)

FRANK: So?

ROGER: It's coming, it's coming.

FRANK: Jesus.

(ROGER *continues pacing for a moment. Then he suddenly stops, faces* FRANK, *and goes into the scene.*)

ROGER: And if you'll just stop talking for a minute you'll see what I mean.

FRANK: I'm not talking.

ROGER: (*Out of the scene*) Not yet, Frank. (*Slight pause. He goes back into the scene.*) It's just that being stuck in this aide role doesn't give me much of a chance, see, even though I'm supposed to be one of the sane ones, one of the ones close to authority. And yet that's just it: so close yet so far away, kind of like I exist only in limbo, only in transit, like all I can do is look at the script from the outside, look at the players dancing and laughing and partying and scheming while I wait to shuffle on from the wings 'cause that's my character, see, that's the way it's been written, been written to keep me from the source of all that power. And maybe that's what it is: power. Sometimes thinking that if I were a powerful person I could just bust a hole in the world and reach in and grab what I wanted.... And so he seemed to say, if you'd only let my eyes absorb you, let me suck you into me, you would be a part of a great power beyond yourself, a power that only I and others like me can really possess. I could do so much for you if you'd only see me for who I am, for what I represent, for how I can....

(ROGER *stares at* FRANK, *stares as though trying to meld with him.* FRANK *waits, not knowing what to do without lines.* RITA *waits, too, watching both men.*)

(*The pause, the stare, the silence hold until they're nearly unbearable. Then just as* FRANK *is finally moved to say something, to act...*)

ROGER: (*Moving away from* FRANK) End of out-take.

FRANK: What?

ROGER: End of scene.

FRANK: That was a scene?

ROGER: Yes.

FRANK: That was a monologue, man. Where the hell were my lines? What were my actions, my objective?

ROGER: You didn't get it.

FRANK: No.

ROGER: You don't remember.

FRANK: What's there to remember? You made it up.

ROGER: Yeah, I made it up.

FRANK: That was weird, Roger. That was really weird.

RITA: Yeah, it gave me the chills.

ROGER: Just an improv. As in freedom. You know, like letting a ball of string unwind until it gets to the end. That kind of unraveling.

FRANK: *(Tentatively)* Okay…

ROGER: But then there's nothing left. You're right. Nothing left. Strung out, so to speak. *(He stares into space.)*

FRANK: Roger?

RITA: *(To FRANK)* I told you.

FRANK: Hush up…. Roger? You okay?

ROGER: Yeah, I'm okay.

FRANK: You wanna lie down or something?

ROGER: No, no. Look, I'm sorry.

FRANK: No, that's all right.

ROGER: I've got all these things racing through my head. My mind is sorta cluttered. Just my way of trying to work through some of it, trying to prepare myself for what lies ahead.

FRANK: Hey, man, it's okay. I understand. It's the world, man. The world on your ass. Bizarreness, weirdness. I understand. Shit, it's a good thing you got out of New York when you did. But like you said, you're safe here. Cocoon-like atmosphere. So just relax. Call it a rest stop. Listen, why don't you do some dope?

RITA: *(Sarcastically)* Oh, now that should really help.

FRANK: Rita! *(To ROGER)* It should help mellow you out a little.

ROGER: No, thanks.

FRANK: How about another drink then?

ROGER: No, I'm fine, really.

FRANK: Well, I could sure use one. Honey, how about getting me a refill?

RITA: *(Hesitantly)* Frank....

(FRANK motions RITA to go. She takes up FRANK's glass and exits into the kitchen. FRANK begins filling the pipe with marijuana and lighting up.)

FRANK: An improv, huh?

ROGER: Yeah, something I've been working on.

FRANK: Working on for who?

ROGER: Myself.

FRANK: But why *Cuckoo's Nest*?

ROGER: 'Cause that's where it all started.

FRANK: What?

ROGER: My gradual shift in focus. My reality check. My journey through *Native Son* and *Titus Andronicus* and *Dutchman*. All the way up to my Camaro...and beyond.

FRANK: *(Not quite understanding)* Yeah, well, I do know all that driving can get you down. Shit, I drive across town and I'm a raving maniac. Fucking asshole people always getting in your way. I'd had it with L A and all the—

ROGER: *(Sharply)* You've told me that already, Frank. You've told me what you've had it with.

FRANK: Yeah, 'cause this country's killing us by the thousands. No more real feelings, no more insights. It's fifties horror movie time. *Invasion of the Body Snatchers*. Shit like that. But I will say one thing—something you probably already know. With most black people it's different.

ROGER: How is it different?

FRANK: At least you're fighting. Just like you said. At least your legacy makes you a part of the anti-world,

the new blood that just might keep the system from
running down completely. If there's any hope for the
next era it's with you and others like you.

ROGER: Is that so?

FRANK: Yeah.

ROGER: But you're not black.

FRANK: Of course, I'm not. But there is such a thing
as orientation, connection. I mean, dig into a Pynchon
novel. Look at...other writers. Look at the lines being
drawn between the Preterit and the Elect. Look at the
endless plots and entanglements. And then look at the
positive riffs from underground, from buried souls that
need to rise up out of the muck. Hell, it's almost like a
jazz thing.

ROGER: *(With attitude)* A black "thang".

FRANK: No. That is...that's not what I mean, dammit.
I'm not talking about digging up old tired clichés. I'm
not talking about that. I'm talking about new energy,
man, positive input. Us. I'm talking about us. About
the need to recognize the interface between us.

*(RITA enters with the gin and tonic just as FRANK and
ROGER seem to be staring into each other's eyes.)*

RITA: Here's your drink, Frank.

FRANK: *(Without looking at her)* Just set it down
somewhere, honey.

*(RITA puts the glass on the coffee table and plops down in
the chair D L.)*

FRANK: Listen to this, Roger: "Somewhere among the
wastes of the world is the key that will bring us back,
restore us to our earth and to our freedom." That's
from Thomas Pynchon's *Gravity's Rainbow*. And I guess
that best describes what I'm trying to do. The key. Find

the fucking key... Look, let me show you some of my work. *(He heads to the exit to the bedrooms.)*

RITA: Frank, don't drag all that stuff out here.

FRANK: I wanna show him.

RITA: It's boring.

FRANK: To you, maybe. *(He exits.)*

RITA: *(To* ROGER*)* It's boring as hell. He's got these stacks of papers all over the bedroom. It's like I can't get to him sometimes for all the paper, all the goddam words. Who needs them?

ROGER: He does.

*(*FRANK *comes in with an armful of papers.)*

FRANK: My notes. *(He sets the papers on the U S table.)* Come here. I wanna show you.

*(*ROGER *goes to the table.)*

FRANK: Like I was saying. A little bit of everything. Months of work, of research.

*(*ROGER *looks through the papers as* FRANK *waits for a response.)*

ROGER: I'm sorry but I can't read too much of this.

FRANK: That's okay.

ROGER: The handwriting.

FRANK: Yeah, never did have real legible handwriting.

RITA: I told him he ought to get a typewriter.

FRANK: I can't type.

RITA: You could learn.

FRANK: Rita, you type, I write. There's a difference.

RITA: Maybe so. But I make money typing, see? Money. I may be typing other people's stuff, but it's my money.

FRANK: Well, that ain't the point now, is it? Typing's not the point.

RITA: You just don't want nobody to really see how stupid your ideas are, that's all.

FRANK: I'm not listening to you right now so just shut up, please. *(To* ROGER*)* Getting any clearer?

ROGER: Some of it.

FRANK: These are just notes. You know, elemental, rudimentary. Absolute clarity's gonna take a while. I need time and space to think, to straighten things out. And once I do I'm gonna blast outta here like a fucking rocket to the moon.

RITA: And what about me?

FRANK: You too, honey.

RITA: Me too, what?

FRANK: You, me, and Roger.

RITA: What do you mean "you, me, and Roger"?

FRANK: We're in this together.

RITA: We ain't in nothing together.

FRANK: Come on, you know what I mean.

RITA: No, I don't know what you mean. Most of the time when you get like this I don't understand you at all.

FRANK: When I get like what?

RITA: You know.

FRANK: *(Shouting)* When I fucking get like what?

RITA: Don't yell at me.

FRANK: *(Shouting)* I'm not yelling. This is my voice, my normal everyday voice. Who the fuck's yelling?

RITA: Well, it's not my fault you didn't make it.

FRANK: Make it?

RITA: As a big star.

FRANK: What are you talking about? *(To* ROGER*)* Do you know what she's talking about? 'Cause I don't know what she's talking about.

RITA: You know damn well what I'm talking about.

FRANK: She hasn't understood a thing I've been saying.

RITA: Shit.

FRANK: She just hasn't got it.

RITA: Yeah, and I don't want it either.

FRANK: She just hasn't got your insight. She misses our connection.

RITA: What connection?

FRANK: She just can't feel the vibrations.

RITA: You're right, I can't.

FRANK: Thank God you dropped by, Roger.

RITA: That's right.

FRANK: Thank God for that.

RITA: Make me invisible.

FRANK: Thank God for good friends who understand.

RITA: Who? Him?

FRANK: Yeah, a fellow artist.

RITA: Shit.

FRANK: Because it's about perception, about the ability to perceive.

RITA: Really?

FRANK: Fucking right.

RITA: All right then. Since you're so smart, so perceptive, just listen to this: I'm not pregnant.

FRANK: What?

RITA: I said I'm not pregnant.

FRANK: Not—

RITA: Pregnant.

FRANK: Not pregnant.

RITA: No.

FRANK: Then what the fuck was—

RITA: It was an act, all an act.

FRANK: An act.

RITA: Yeah. I did it. And I was great.

FRANK: All an act.

RITA: I knew I could do it. Now just go ahead and ignore me now.

FRANK: You're kidding.

RITA: If you think so.

FRANK: You mean you were just pretending?

RITA: No, Frank, sweetheart. I was acting. Acting!

FRANK: What the hell difference does it make?

RITA: A lot. A hell of a lot. I can pretend by myself. I can pretend without thinking, without planning. I used to do it all the time when I was a kid. But this was acting—in front of somebody. In front of you.

FRANK: Why you sneaky little—

RITA: Uh-uh-uh. Actress. I am an actress.

FRANK: Oh, yeah?

RITA: Yeah. As good as you.

FRANK: Shit.

RITA: You fell for it. The perfect audience. You fell for the whole thing.

FRANK: *(To* ROGER*)* I knew it all the time.

RITA: Like hell you did.

FRANK: I did. I really did. It was me who was acting.

RITA: That wasn't acting, honey, that was real.

FRANK: Just great acting.

RITA: Real afraid, not pretend afraid.

FRANK: *(To* ROGER*)* She'll never learn, will she?

RITA: Learn what? Will you talk to me! Will you just talk to me!

FRANK: About real acting.

RITA: I learned enough to do a number on you.

FRANK: When are you gonna get it through your thick skull that I was just humoring you?

RITA: Yeah, you were funny all right.

FRANK: Just playing along.

RITA: You're just jealous, that's all.

FRANK: Jealous?

RITA: Yeah, jealous. For the first time I beat you, Frank Tracy. You with your books and words and places you've been and people you've met and plays you've been in. You! And you can't stand it. You won't give an inch. You won't admit that I beat you. That I can act too when I want to. You're nothing but an egotistical piece of shit, Frank. All you. Always you, you, you. And I hate it. All this pretense. All this bullshit. I hate it.

FRANK: *(Reaching out to her)* Rita, honey.

RITA: Stay away from me.

FRANK: I'm sorry.

RITA: The hell you are.

FRANK: Honey, listen.

RITA: Go talk to Roger. He'll listen to you. *(She exits D L into the bedrooms.)*

FRANK: Well, I'll be damned. You know she's right. She really had me fooled. I've got to hand it to her.

ROGER: Don't you think she deserves to fool you?

(FRANK is taken aback for a moment.)

FRANK: Hey, now wait a minute. Let me just explain this situation to you, okay? You see, me and Rita need each other to survive in this town. It's need, man. Hell, she's the only real person for miles. The rest are zombies. They walk around like the only thing behind their eyes is dead air. So I need her. And she needs me, too. It's just that she doesn't know sometimes—doesn't understand. My ideas scare her, make her wanna put on earmuffs. But hell, I can't blame her really. She grew up in a town down the road a tenth the size of this shithole. Her mother's dead, her brother stares at automobile parts in Detroit, and her father's a drunk. A real drunk. And she's scared that I'm gonna turn out like him.

ROGER: And of course you don't think you will.

(Once again FRANK is taken aback.)

ROGER: Why are you here, Frank?

FRANK: I already told you why.

ROGER: Oh, you feel persecuted, pursued. You wanna kick around like some wasted black jazz musician doing riffs in some funky little dive because his heart, his life, his soul's at stake. Is that it?

FRANK: No, that's not it.

ROGER: What then?

FRANK: I told you. I want to be free. I want to be free to make my own choices, my own world. I've got things I want to do, things I want to say, and I can't if there's a million people on my back.

ROGER: No, of course you can't. 'Cause you ain't "the man." Not really.

FRANK: Look, I don't know about you, but I can't mask the death and destruction. Uh-uh. I can't pretend. I can't flatten things out into some pale, sedate, white... that's right, white sense of a world blown into easy numbness by fear and sameness.

ROGER: Look who's talking about fear.

FRANK: Yeah, well, there's all kinds of fear, you know.

ROGER: I know. I know there's all kinds of fear.... All right, then act. As in "move", that is. Keep moving, keep fighting.

FRANK: I am fighting.

ROGER: No, you've retreated.

FRANK: From acting.

ROGER: From the world.

FRANK: From the business. From doing a dance. From the business of doing a dance. I'm through, finished. It's over. No more fucking strings over this man's head. No more puppet action. No more dancing in Zombie-land.

ROGER: And what do you call this here?

FRANK: Look, if you can't see what I'm saying then that's fine with me. If you want to pursue bullshit for the rest of your life then that's just fine with me.

ROGER: That's not what I want.

FRANK: Well, I can only go by what I see.

ROGER: Then why don't you take a good look at yourself?

(FRANK *gives* ROGER *a hard stare.*)

FRANK: And why don't you just leave, huh? Shit, I thought that you of all people would at least understand me. What'd you stop here for anyway? To look me over? To spit in my face? What? Why don't you just go on out to the Coast in your kick-ass convertible like you're the fucking black Red Baron and—

(Suddenly, music blasts from the bedroom. RITA *has put on Janis Joplin's "Try, Just a Little Bit Harder.")*

FRANK: *(Yelling)* Rita, will you turn that shit down!

(Music continues to blast.)

FRANK: Rita! …Sonofabitch.

(FRANK *heads D L toward the exit to the bedrooms and exits. In his frustration* ROGER *lets out an ear-piercing scream as the music continues to blast. Then he goes to his shoulder bag and takes out a gun. Facing D S, he looks at it for a moment, then looks up.)*

(Music stops abruptly and ROGER *quickly puts the gun away and puts his bag down in plain view on the coffee table. As* FRANK *and* RITA *begin to argue offstage,* ROGER *shakes out his arms as though loosening up, then pushes a breath of air out of his lungs. He now appears calmer, more confident, in some ways transformed.)*

(FRANK *and* RITA's *arguing stops, and they eventually come in speaking more calmly.)*

FRANK: *(Offstage)* Look, honey, I know how you feel.

RITA: *(Offstage)* Skin to skin, Frank. You hear me? It's skin to skin.

FRANK: I know, honey, I know…. All better now, Rog.

(ROGER *continues to face D S.* FRANK *laughs, then speaks with a spot-on, playfully lilting Irish brogue.)*

FRANK: Still stuck in the ole "Cuckoo's Nest," are we?

(ROGER *continues facing D S.)*

FRANK: *(Back to his "regular" voice)* That was a joke.

ROGER: *(Still facing D S)* He had gray eyes.

FRANK: Who did?

(ROGER *finally turns to* FRANK *and* RITA.*)*

ROGER: I'd like for you and Rita to sit down for a minute or so, Frank. Sit down and listen to me for a minute or so.

FRANK: But what—

ROGER: *(With seemingly uncharacteristic resolve)* Sit down! ...Please, just sit down.

(FRANK *and* RITA *sit down on the sofa, the shoulder bag conspicuously before them.)*

ROGER: I met him at this party at an apartment off Central Park. One of those places where each floor is one apartment. Just that big. I didn't know a soul there except for Madeline, the woman I went with. She had wangled an invitation from a friend of a friend and there we were, this mixed couple who had just finished doing *Dutchman* off-off-Broadway. Huh, Clay and Lula decked out as best we could and ready to enter this party given by somebody whose name we hadn't even heard of before that night. This prim-looking guy took our coats and we squirmed into this warm vat of beautiful people like baby eels. And after just fifteen minutes, me standing alone at a table filled with food because I was hungry as hell, I saw him staring at me. I knew right then what was happening, and I thought: I've been in New York for eight years and I came to this party for some reason so what am I getting so

nervous about? ...He called me up and we had lunch.
I didn't tell Madeline about my fortune. I didn't tell
anybody. I was going to go it alone. Protecting my
interests, my reputation. He was my height and very
relaxed and his hair was thinning and I felt nervous
and we talked bullshit and he said he might could do
things for me 'cause he'd actually seen me in a couple
of shows and I said terrific and then suddenly thought:
it's like being a fish.... I took the train to Westchester,
and he met me at the station, dressed casually, smiling.
What a smile. It was priceless.... It was Sunday
afternoon. Really bright and sunny. The air was like
laughing gas it was so different from New York's.
And there was this silence, this fundamental silence.
At first I connected it with my parents' neighborhood
and I got this sudden chill. Then I connected it with
this bubble I've been living in for more than twenty
years that people tend to take for something like quiet
intelligence or contemplative seriousness or diluted
blackness and that made me a little queasy. And
then I remembered that he was talking to me about
stupid shit like what we were going to have for dinner
and I felt a little numb. *(Slight pause)* I'm sitting...
sitting on this sofa in a dark-paneled den wrapped in
bookshelves and paintings and pictures of people "in
the business," as they say. I'm sitting there, I'm sitting
there, see, when suddenly the lights dim a little. I look
up and see him coming toward the sofa, smiling. Jesus,
what a smile. And he's carrying two glasses of brandy.
This after shrimp cocktail and roast beef German style
and baked potatoes and salad and wine and coffee.
And my head's swimming with all the things he's been
telling me about his life and about his work. Stories,
anecdotes, dirty little jokes. He gives me a brandy and
sits next to me on the sofa and we toast to my future
success. We put our glasses down on the table and
he tells me how glad he is that I've come and I tell

him that I really appreciate his hospitality and then
this silence seems to hit both of us over the head like
hammer. He smiles again, smiles for the longest time,
and I think: that smile really has nothing to do with
me, with who I actually am, that is. It's as blind as a
bat.... I see a quick gleam in those gray eyes of his.
It's something new, something...kinda desperate. I
hold my breath. And in the instant between that flash
of light and his placing his hand on the back of my
neck I think about the people who give up a part of
themselves as the key to opening some certain door,
and I want to join them on that other side, want to be
a part of something beyond myself. But the touch of
his hand sends this chill down my spine like a bolt of
lightening and I knock it away quickly, instinctively....
It's the first time I've ever seen him annoyed, angry.
I let out a nervous little laugh and say: "Every other
person in this country either wants your money or
your ass." And do you know what he does? He laughs.
He just rears his head back and laughs. And I see
through that laughter a cheap, slimy, manipulative
little white man who just knows he's got one more
nigger by the balls. My eyes get hot and teary and
something seems to explode inside my head and I hit
him in the face as hard as I've hit anything or anybody
in my life. And I keep hitting him, knocking his head
back and forth like it's a pink punching bag until my
knuckles get sore and his head just seems to dangle
over the arm of the sofa like a slab of rancid meat.
(*Slight pause*) I've been killing people all my life, but I
never thought it would ever actually happen.

RITA: Oh, my God.

(*For the first time* FRANK *seems genuinely stunned.*)

RITA: Frank, we've got to do something.

(ROGER *seems to recover, to come back to himself from some far-off place.*)

ROGER: Now it's your turn, Frank. Tell us a story. And make it real, make it true. Tell us the story about the time I tried to kill you.

(FRANK *thinks for a moment and then suddenly surmises what* ROGER *must be talking about.*)

FRANK: That wasn't real, Roger.

RITA: When?

FRANK: That was fake.

ROGER: I was serious.

RITA: He tried to kill you?

FRANK: No.

ROGER: Yes.

FRANK: It was a mistake.

ROGER: An excuse.

FRANK: You just got carried away.

RITA: When?

FRANK: A rehearsal.

ROGER: My hands around your neck.

RITA: He choked you?

FRANK: Just a rehearsal.

ROGER: They had to pull me off of you.

FRANK: An intense rehearsal, that's all.

ROGER: I wanted you dead.

FRANK: No, you didn't.

ROGER: Why won't you face it?

FRANK: Because it isn't true.

ROGER: Tell her why.

FRANK: There's no "why".

ROGER: Tell her why it happened.

FRANK: It didn't happen.

ROGER: Tell her dammit!

(Pause)

FRANK: It was nothing, Rita. Nothing.

(RITA *and* ROGER *simply wait.*)

FRANK: A kiss, that's all. Just a hug and a kiss.

ROGER: "Just."

FRANK: Just a little fascination, that's all. Envy.

ROGER: Whatever you say.

FRANK: I was drunk, delirious.

ROGER: You scared me to death.

FRANK: *(To* RITA*)* It was such a little thing.

ROGER: And each night in *Cuckoo's Nest*, when I had
to drag you down and subdue you, it was like I was
trying to kill you. Not because I hated you, but because
I hated myself for how much I was drawn to you, to
your sense of power and abandon.

FRANK: But it wasn't real, Roger. I was acting.

ROGER: When? When were you acting?

(FRANK *is suddenly at a loss for words, curiously stumped
by* ROGER's *question.*)

ROGER: You know, even in the end, when Hank and
I would wheel lobotomized you in on that gurney in
front of Nurse Ratchet, in front of all those crazies, I
knew that you had won, had triumphed. And it was all
I could do to take my eyes off you and leave the stage.

FRANK: Roger, I—

ROGER: And when the lights would fade on *Cuckoo's Nest* and it would be all over for the moment and we'd all be backstage and you'd be laughing and joking like it was nothing, like it was a piece of cake, I'd sneak a look at my hands... *(Looking at his hands)* ...at my black hands, and see them sweating and shaking with rage and fear and wonder what I could do with it all, where I could put it. *(Looking at* FRANK *again)* Why don't you do me a little favor now, Frank. Do your "good buddy" a little favor. Tell me I win. Tell me I win this time.

FRANK: Win? Win what? What the fuck are you talking about? You ain't win nothing. You just stepped in it. Stepped in it nice and good. Right on up to your neck in it.

*(*ROGER *waits in frustration just a moment longer. Then he goes to his shoulder bag and takes out the gun.)*

RITA: Oh, my God!

ROGER: Tell me I win, Frank.

FRANK: Oh, well, now that's slick. That's really slick.

RITA: Please, don't kill him, Roger.

ROGER: Stay out of this, Rita. *(To* FRANK*)* I win, right?

*(*FRANK *says nothing.)*

RITA: Tell him yes, Frank.

ROGER: I said stay out of this, Rita. *(Cocking the gun)* Right?!

RITA: *(Gasping)* Oh, God!

(Slight pause)

FRANK: All right, Roger. You've got the power now. You've got the fucking power. So I guess you win.

ROGER: *(Uncocking and lowering the gun)* Fucking right... One more thing, Frank.

(ROGER *goes to his shoulder bag and takes out a framed 8 X 10 photograph and gives it to* FRANK. *It's a picture of* FRANK *and the producer, who has an arm around* FRANK'*s shoulders.*)

FRANK: Where'd you get this?

ROGER: I sorta lifted it from his den. You and him at some party. Arms around each other.

FRANK: Morris Hathaway?

ROGER: Yeah, all post *Easy Rider* and shit.

FRANK: Oh, man. *(Slight pause)* There're so many kinds of deals, Roger. So many tiny little ways to be corrupted. Pretty soon you lose count. That movie never led to anything anyway. Not really. Things often lead to nothing. You must have learned that by now. Haven't you at least learned that? Things often lead to nothing.

ROGER: Or something. Like with your Social Security scheme.

(FRANK *looks back and forth between* RITA *and* ROGER.)

FRANK: Look…I…on the Coast…on the Coast I was in a trance most of the time. Either that or drunk. And when I was working it was like I was…. I don't know. And then one day I woke up and found myself here. Back where I started. In the middle of the country. Where a view of the ocean is just another wet dream.

(FRANK *lets out a short laugh, but* RITA *and* ROGER *are silent.*)

FRANK: Look, I was born here, dammit. Right in this house. Right in that bedroom back there. Popping out of my mom before my dad even had a chance to get his shoes on. So it's sorta like a place for me to begin again. And I've got to begin again. It's the only way.

(ROGER *recognizes the depth of honesty in what* FRANK *has finally admitted. He places the gun on the coffee table.*)

RITA: Frank, get the police. Call them. Call somebody.

ROGER: You don't wanna call nobody, do you, Frank? You just wanna get closer to that feeling, that freedom in the soul. Whatever it is. Whatever you think it is. Writing and talking yourself into oblivion looking for it.

FRANK: You been looking for it, too.

(ROGER *takes in what* FRANK *has said, acknowledging the true in it. Then...*)

ROGER: *(Quoting)* "In the darkness his fear made live in him an element which he reckoned with as 'them.'"

(FRANK *is slightly puzzled.*)

ROGER: *Native Son.*

RITA: Frank, get the gun. Get it.

FRANK: No, it's all right.

RITA: Are you out of your mind?

FRANK: I tell you it's all right.

(*Impulsively,* RITA *rushes to the coffee table and picks up the gun, pointing it at* ROGER.)

RITA: *(Shaking with fear)* All right, you son of a bitch.

FRANK: What the hell are you doing, Rita?

RITA: Just get the hell outta here.

FRANK: Put that damn thing down before you hurt yourself.

RITA: Who asked you to come here anyway?

ROGER: Nobody.

RITA: Then just go. We don't need you.

ROGER: But what about Janis and Smokey?

(ROGER *makes a gesture toward* RITA *that causes her to pull the trigger, almost as a nervous reaction. The gun fires. It scares the hell out of* FRANK *and* RITA. *But* ROGER *barely reacts.* RITA *stares at the gun, shocked and confused.*)

FRANK: Jesus Christ!

ROGER: It's a prop gun, a starter pistol.

(FRANK *takes the gun from* RITA *and places it and the photograph on the coffee table. Then he comforts her.*)

RITA: (*Shaken*) My God, Frank, my God.

(ROGER *gets his bag and drapes it over his shoulder. Then he looks around the room.*)

ROGER: You know, I got off the highway on the "other" side of town—literally across the tracks. I was so lost. Got directions from this black service station attendant. Caught the look in his eyes. Kinda like: you sure you wanna go there, Brotherman? ...I followed the little map he'd sketched for me on a napkin and watched the complexion of this town change right before my eyes. And I thought: it's like the Sirens. The Sirens. When will these Sirens stop singing in my head? ...You see, I want to believe you, Frank. I really do want to believe that we exist in the same space. I really do want to believe in your...interface. But not at the expense of the freedom in my soul. (*Slight pause*) I'd better be heading out. I need to see California real soon. Gotta see the Pacific Ocean. Wanna sit on top of one of those sand dunes I've heard so much about and look out over the Pacific like it's the edge of the world. Hell, might could one day even be a star. (*Looking specifically at* RITA) Or at least a comet.

FRANK: But what about Hathaway?

ROGER: What about him?

(FRANK *just looks at* ROGER *for a moment.*)

FRANK: Sonofabitch. You…you didn't kill him, did you?

ROGER: *(With a wry smile)* Well, let me see now, Frank. Which answer would make me the least crazy?

(FRANK *can't say.*)

(ROGER *continues looking at* FRANK, *this time with a kind of kinship that, despite himself, he knows he'll never ever be able to let go of.*)

ROGER: I gotta thank you, Frank. Thank you with all my heart.

FRANK: Thank me for what?

ROGER: For being here… *(Gesturing to his head)* in my head, I mean…all this time.

(ROGER *exits, closing the door behind him,* FRANK *looking after him. Then* FRANK *turns back to* RITA. *They just look at each other, the gun and the photograph conspicuously on the table between them.*)

(*Music rises slowly. It's Steely Dan's* Home at Last.)

(*Lights fade to black.*)

END OF PLAY